Contents

Guidance

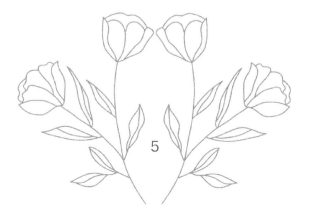

1

آهْدِنَا ٱلصِّرَاطَ ٱلْمُسْتَقِيمَ

Ihdinas-Siraatal-Mustaqeem

"Guide us on the straight path."

Qur'an 1:6

A du'a asking for guidance onto the straight path

2

رَبَّنَا وَلَا تَحْمِلْ عَلَيْنَآ إِصْرًا كَمَا حَمَلْتَهُ عَلَى ٱلَّذِينَ مِن قَبْلِنَا

Rabbana wa laa tahmil-'alainaaa isran kamaa hamaltahoo 'alal-lazeena min qablinaa

"Our Lord, and lay not upon us a burden like that which You laid upon those before us."

Qur'an 2:286

A du'a asking Allah (swt) to make it easier for us to be upon the path of righteousness

3

رَبَّنَا فَٱغْفِرْ لَنَا ذُنُوبَنَا وَكَفِّرْ عَنَّا سَيِّئَاتِنَا وَتَوَفَّنَا مَعَ ٱلْأَبْرَارِ

*Rabbanaa faghfir lanaa zunoobanaa
wa kaffir 'annaa saiyi aatina wa
tawaffanaa ma'al abraar*

"Our Lord, so forgive us our sins and
remove from us our misdeeds and
cause us to die among the righteous."

Qur'an 3:193

A dua'a for repentance and asking
Allah (swt) to take us while we are
guided on the right path

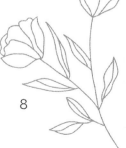

4

لَئِن لَّمۡ يَهۡدِنِى رَبِّى لَأَكُونَنَّ مِنَ ٱلۡقَوۡمِ ٱلضَّآلِّينَ

*la'il lam yahdinee Rabbee la
akoonanna minal qawmid daaalleen*

"Unless my Lord guides me, I will surely
be among the people gone astray."

Qur'an 6:77

A dua'a asking Allah (swt) for
guidance

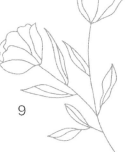

5

وَٱتَّبِعْ مَا يُوحَىٰٓ إِلَيْكَ وَٱصْبِرْ حَتَّىٰ يَحْكُمَ ٱللَّهُ ۚ وَهُوَ خَيْرُ
ٱلْحَٰكِمِينَ

Wattabi' maa yoohaaa ilaika wasbir hattaa yahkumal laah; wa Huwa khairul haakimeen

"And follow what is revealed to you, [O Muhammad], and be patient until Allah will judge. And He is the best of judges."

Qur'an 10:109

A dua'a for guidance

6

عَسَىٰٓ أَن يَهْدِيَنِ رَبِّى لِأَقْرَبَ مِنْ هَٰذَا رَشَدًا

*Asaaa any yahdiyani Rabbee li
aqraba min haazaa rashadaa*

"Perhaps my Lord will guide me to
what is nearer than this to right
conduct."

Qur'an 18:24

A dua'a asking for Allah's (swt)
guidance

Faith

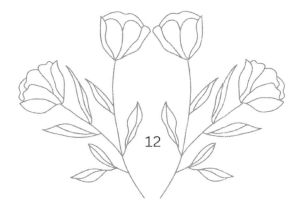

1

وَٱسْتَعِينُوا۟ بِٱلصَّبْرِ وَٱلصَّلَوٰةِ ۚ وَإِنَّهَا لَكَبِيرَةٌ إِلَّا عَلَى ٱلْخَٰشِعِينَ ٱلَّذِينَ يَظُنُّونَ أَنَّهُم مُّلَٰقُوا۟ رَبِّهِمْ وَأَنَّهُمْ إِلَيْهِ رَٰجِعُونَ

Wasta'eenoo bissabri was Salaah; wa innahaa lakabee ratun illaa alal khaashi'een Allazeena yazunnoona annahum mulaaqoo Rabbihim wa annahum ilaihi raaji'oon

"And seek help through patience and prayer, and indeed, it is difficult except for the humbly submissive [to Allah swt] Who are certain that they will meet their Lord and that they will return to Him."

Qur'an 2:45-46

A du'a for renewal of faith

2

رَبَّنَا وَٱجْعَلْنَا مُسْلِمَيْنِ لَكَ وَمِن ذُرِّيَّتِنَا أُمَّةً مُّسْلِمَةً لَّكَ وَأَرِنَا مَنَاسِكَنَا
وَتُبْ عَلَيْنَا إِنَّكَ أَنتَ ٱلتَّوَّابُ ٱلرَّحِيمُ

*Rabbana waj'alnaa muslimaini laka wa min
zurriyyatinaaa ummatam muslimatal laka wa
arinaa manaasikanaa wa tub 'alainaa innaka
antat Tawwaabur Raheem*

"Our Lord, and make us Muslims [in
submission] to You and from our descendants
a Muslim nation [in submission] to You. And
show us our rites [of worship] and accept our
repentance. Indeed, You are the Accepting
of Repentance, the Merciful."

Qur'an 2:128

A du'a to affirm your faith in Islam

14

3

رَبَّنَآ إِنَّكَ جَامِعُ ٱلنَّاسِ لِيَوْمٍ لَّا رَيْبَ فِيهِ إِنَّ ٱللَّهَ لَا يُخْلِفُ ٱلْمِيعَادَ

Rabbanaaa innaka jaami 'un-naasil Yawmil laa raibafeeh; innal laaha laa yukhliful mee'aad

"Our Lord, surely You will gather the people for a Day about which there is no doubt. Indeed, Allah does not fail in His promise."

Qur'an 3:9

A dua'a to affirm your faith in the afterlife

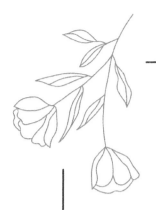

4

رَبَّنَآ ءَامَنَّا بِمَآ أَنزَلْتَ وَٱتَّبَعْنَا ٱلرَّسُولَ فَٱكْتُبْنَا مَعَ ٱلشَّٰهِدِينَ

Rabbanaaa aamannaa bimaaa anzalta wattaba'nar Rasoola faktubnaa ma'ash shaahideen

"Our Lord, we have believed in what You revealed and have followed the messenger [i.e., Jesus], so register us among the witnesses [to truth]."

Qur'an 3:53

A dua'a of faith and worship

5

رَبَّنَآ إِنَّنَا سَمِعْنَا مُنَادِيًا يُنَادِي لِلْإِيمَنِ أَنْ ءَامِنُوا بِرَبِّكُمْ فَآمَنَّا

Rabbanaaa innanaa sami'naa munaadiyai
yunaadee lil eemaani an aaminoo bi
Rabbikum fa aamannaa

"Our Lord, indeed we have heard a caller,
calling to faith, [saying], 'Believe in your Lord,'
and we have believed."

Qur'an 3:193

A dua'a of humility, submission and faith

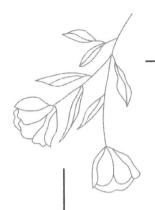

6

رَبَّنَآ ءَامَنَّا فَٱكْتُبْنَا مَعَ ٱلشَّـٰهِدِينَ

Rabbanaaa aamannaa faktubnaa
ma'ash shaahideen

"Our Lord, we have believed, so
register us among the witnesses."

Qur'an 5:83

A dua'a for those who want to testify
the truth and verbally affirm their
belief in it

7

رَبِّ ٱغْفِرْ لِى وَلِأَخِى وَأَدْخِلْنَا فِى رَحْمَتِكَ ۖ وَأَنتَ أَرْحَمُ ٱلرَّ'حِمِينَ

Rabbighfirlee wa li akhee wa adkhilnaa fee rahmatika wa Anta arhamur raahimeen

"My Lord, forgive me and my brother and admit us into Your mercy, for You are the most merciful of the merciful."

Qur'an 7:151

A dua'a for believers

8

إِنَّمَا يَأْتِيكُم بِهِ ٱللَّهُ إِن شَآءَ وَمَآ أَنتُم بِمُعْجِزِينَ

Innamaa yaateekum bihil laahu in shaaa'a
wa maaa antum bimu'jizeen

"Allah will only bring it to you if He wills, and
you will not cause [Him] failure."

Qur'an 11:33

A dua'a asking Allah (swt) for steadfastness
in religion

9

رَبِّ قَدْ ءَاتَيْتَنِى مِنَ ٱلْمُلْكِ وَعَلَّمْتَنِى مِن تَأْوِيلِ ٱلْأَحَادِيثِ ۚ فَاطِرَ
ٱلسَّمَٰوَٰتِ وَٱلْأَرْضِ أَنتَ وَلِىِّ فِى ٱلدُّنْيَا وَٱلْءَاخِرَةِ ۖ تَوَفَّنِى مُسْلِمًا وَأَلْحِقْنِى
بِٱلصَّٰلِحِينَ

*Rabbi qad aataitanee minal mulki wa
'allamtanee min taaweelil ahaadees; faati
ras samaawaati wal ardi Anta waliyyee fid
dunyaa wal Aakhirati tawaffanee
muslimanw wa alhiqnee bissaaliheen*

"My Lord, You have given me [something]
of sovereignty and taught me of the
interpretation of dreams. Creator of the
heavens and earth, You are my protector
in this world and in the Hereafter. Cause
me to die a Muslim and join me with the
righteous."

Qur'an 12:101

A dua'a for strong faith

10

وَلَهُۥ مَا فِى ٱلسَّمَٰوَٰتِ وَٱلْأَرْضِ وَلَهُ ٱلدِّينُ وَاصِبًاۚ

Wa lahoo maa fis samaawaati wal
ardi wa lahud deenu waasibaa

"And to Him belongs whatever is in
the heavens and the earth, and to
Him is [due] worship constantly."

Qur'an 16:52

A dua'a asking Allah (swt) for
steadfastness in religion

Children

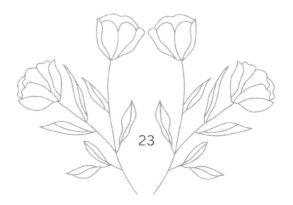

1

بَدِيعُ ٱلسَّمَٰوَٰتِ وَٱلۡأَرۡضِ ۖ وَإِذَا قَضَىٰٓ أَمۡرٗا فَإِنَّمَا يَقُولُ لَهُۥ كُن فَيَكُونُ

Badeee'us samaawaati wal ardi wa izaa qadaaa amran fa innamaa yaqoolu lahoo kun fayakoon

"Originator of the heavens and the earth. When He decrees a matter, He only says to it, "Be," and it is."

Qur'an 2:117

A du'a for offspring

2

رَبِّ هَبْ لِى مِن لَّدُنكَ ذُرِّيَّةً طَيِّبَةً ۖ إِنَّكَ سَمِيعُ ٱلدُّعَآءِ

Rabbi hab lee mil ladunka zurriyyatan taiyibatan innaka samee'ud du'aaa'

"My Lord, grant me from Yourself a good offspring. Indeed, You are the Hearer of supplication."

Qur'an 3:38

A dua'a asking Allah (swt) for good offspring

3

ٱللَّهُ خَٰلِقُ كُلِّ شَىْءٍ وَهُوَ ٱلْوَٰحِدُ ٱلْقَهَّٰرُ

*Al laahu Khaaliqu kulli shai'inw wa
Huwal Waahidul Qahhar*

"Allah is the Creator of all things,
and He is the One, the Prevailing."

Qur'an 13:16

A dua'a for offspring

4

رَبِّ لَا تَذَرْنِى فَرْدًا وَأَنتَ خَيْرُ ٱلْوَٰرِثِينَ

*Rabbi laa tazarnee fardanw wa
Anta khairul waariseen*

"My Lord, do not leave me alone
[with no heir], while you are the best
of inheritors."

Qur'an 21:89

A dua'a for children

5

رَبَّنَا هَبْ لَنَا مِنْ أَزْوَاجِنَا وَذُرِّيَّتِنَا قُرَّةَ أَعْيُنٍ وَاجْعَلْنَا لِلْمُتَّقِينَ إِمَامًا

Rabbanaa hab lanaa min azwaajinaa wa zurriyaatinaa qurrata a'yuninw waj 'alnaa lilmuttaqeena Imaamaa

"Our Lord, grant us from among our wives and offspring comfort to our eyes and make us a leader [i.e., example] for the righteous."

Qur'an 25:74

A du'a asking Allah (swt) for calmness, joy or happiness among our spouses and through our children and future generations and to be a good leader and role model for the righteous

6

رَبِّ هَبْ لِى مِنَ ٱلصَّٰلِحِينَ

Rabbi hab lee minas saaliheen

"My Lord, grant me [a child] from among the righteous."

Qur'an 37:100

A du'a asking for righteous children

Parents

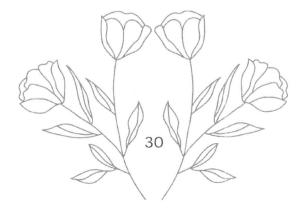

1

رَبَّنَا ٱغْفِرْ لِى وَلِوَٰلِدَىَّ وَلِلْمُؤْمِنِينَ يَوْمَ يَقُومُ ٱلْحِسَابُ

*Rabbanagh fir lee wa liwaalidaiya
wa lilmu'mineena Yawma yaqoomul
hisaab*

"Our Lord, forgive me and my
parents and the believers the Day
the account is established."

Qur'an 14:41

A dua'a asking Allah (swt) to forgive
us and our parents

2

رَّبِّ ٱرْحَمْهُمَا كَمَا رَبَّيَانِى صَغِيرًا

*Rabbir hamhumaa kamaa
rabbayaanee sagheera*

"My Lord, have mercy upon them as
they brought me up [when I was]
small."

Qur'an 17:24

A dua'a asking Allah (swt) to show
mercy to our parents

3

رَبِّ أَوْزِعْنِيٓ أَنْ أَشْكُرَ نِعْمَتَكَ الَّتِيٓ أَنْعَمْتَ عَلَىَّ وَعَلَىٰ وَٰلِدَىَّ وَأَنْ أَعْمَلَ صَٰلِحًا تَرْضَىٰهُ وَأَصْلِحْ لِى فِى ذُرِّيَّتِيٓ إِنِّى تُبْتُ إِلَيْكَ وَإِنِّى مِنَ الْمُسْلِمِينَ

Rabbi awzi' neee an ashkura ni'matakal lateee an'amta 'alaiya wa 'alaa waalidaiya wa an a'mala saalihan tardaahu wa aslih lee fee zurriyyatee; innee tubtu ilaika wa innee minal muslimeen

"My Lord, enable me to be grateful for Your favor which You have bestowed upon me and upon my parents and to work righteousness of which You will approve and make righteous for me my offspring. Indeed, I have repented to You, and indeed, I am of the Muslims."

Qur'an 46:15

A du'a for our parents

4

رَّبِّ ٱغْفِرْ لِى وَلِوَٰلِدَىَّ وَلِمَن دَخَلَ بَيْتِىَ مُؤْمِنًا وَلِلْمُؤْمِنِينَ وَٱلْمُؤْمِنَٰتِ وَلَا تَزِدِ ٱلظَّٰلِمِينَ إِلَّا تَبَارًا

Rabbigh fir lee wa liwaa lidaiya wa liman dakhala baitiya mu'minanw wa lil mu'mineena wal mu'minaati wa laa tazidiz zaalimeena illaa tabaaraa

"My Lord, forgive me and my parents and whoever enters my house a believer and the believing men and believing women. And do not increase the wrongdoers except in destruction."

Qur'an 71:28

A du'a asking for Allah (swt) to forgive our parents

34

Acceptance

of

Deeds

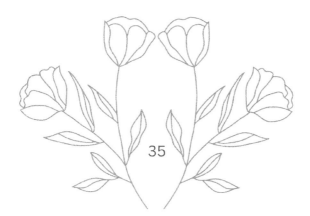

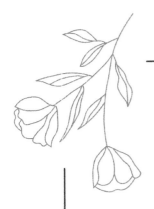

1

رَبَّنَا تَقَبَّلْ مِنَّا إِنَّكَ أَنتَ ٱلسَّمِيعُ ٱلْعَلِيمُ

*Rabbana taqabbal minnaa innaka
Antas Samee'ul Aleem*

"Our Lord, accept [this] from us.
Indeed You are the Hearing, the
Knowing."

Qur'an 2:127

A du'a for whenever you want Allah
(swt) to accept whatever good you
have done

2

رَبِّ ٱجْعَلْنِى مُقِيمَ ٱلصَّلَوٰةِ وَمِن ذُرِّيَّتِى ۚ رَبَّنَا وَتَقَبَّلْ دُعَآءِ

Rabbij 'alnee muqeemas Salaati wa min zurriyyatee Rabbanaa wa taqabbal du'aaa

"My Lord, make me an establisher of prayer, and [many] from my descendants. Our Lord, and accept my supplication."

Qur'an 14:40

A dua'a asking Allah (swt) to make us, and future generations good Muslims and to hear and accept our supplication

3

إِنَّمَا نُطْعِمُكُمْ لِوَجْهِ ٱللَّهِ لَا نُرِيدُ مِنكُمْ جَزَآءً وَلَا شُكُورًا إِنَّا نَخَافُ مِن رَّبِّنَا يَوْمًا عَبُوسًا قَمْطَرِيرًا

Innaamaa nut'imukum li wajhil laahi laa nureedu minkum jazaaa'anw wa laa shukooraa Innaa nakhaafu mir Rabbinna Yawman 'aboosan qamtareeraa

"We feed you only for the countenance of Allah. We wish not from you reward or gratitude. Indeed, We fear from our Lord a Day austere and distressful."

Qur'an 76:9-10

A du'a for the acceptance of charity

Dua'a for Loved Ones

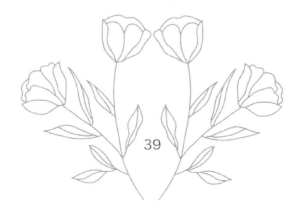

1

أَيْنَ مَا تَكُونُوا يَأْتِ بِكُمُ ٱللَّهُ جَمِيعًا

Ayna maa takoonoo yaati bikumullaahu jamee'aa

"Wherever you may be, Allah (swt) will bring you forth [for judgement] all together."

Qur'an 2:148

A du'a to be united with loved ones

2

بَل سَوَّلَتْ لَكُمْ أَنفُسُكُمْ أَمْرًا فَصَبْرٌ جَمِيلٌ عَسَى ٱللَّهُ أَن يَأْتِيَنِى بِهِمْ جَمِيعًا إِنَّهُ هُوَ ٱلْعَلِيمُ ٱلْحَكِيمُ

Bal sawwalat lakum anfusukum amran fasabrun jameelun 'asal laahu any yaa tiyanee bihim jamee'aa; innahoo Huwal 'Aleemul Hakeem

"Rather, your souls have enticed you to something, so patience is most fitting. Perhaps Allah will bring them to me all together. Indeed it is He who is the Knowing, the Wise."

Qur'an 12:83

A dua'a to be united with loved ones

3

رَبِّ نَجِّنِى وَأَهْلِى مِمَّا يَعْمَلُونَ

Rabbi najjjinee wa ahlee mimmmaa ya'maloon

"My Lord! Save me and my family from what they do."

Qur'an 26:169

A du'a asking Allah (swt) for protection

The Afterlife

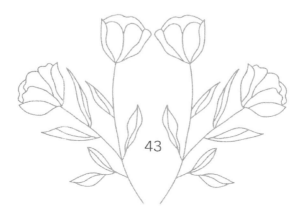

1

رَبَّنَآ ءَاتِنَا فِى ٱلدُّنْيَا حَسَنَةً وَفِى ٱلْءَاخِرَةِ حَسَنَةً وَقِنَا عَذَابَ ٱلنَّارِ

Rabbana atina fid dunyaa hasanatanw wa fil aakhirati hasanatanw wa qinaa azaaban Naar

"Our Lord, give us in this world [that which is] good and in the Hereafter [that which is] good and protect us from the punishment of the Fire."

Qur'an 2:201

A du'a asking for Allah (swt) to grant you good in this world but also the Akhira

2

رَبَّنَآ إِنَّكَ جَامِعُ ٱلنَّاسِ لِيَوۡمٍ لَّا رَيۡبَ فِيهِ إِنَّ ٱللَّهَ لَا يُخۡلِفُ ٱلۡمِيعَادَ

Rabbanaaa innaka jaami 'un-naasil Yawmil laa raibafeeh; innal laaha laa yukhliful mee'aad

"Our Lord, surely You will gather the people for a Day about which there is no doubt. Indeed, Allah does not fail in His promise."

Qur'an 3:9

A dua'a to affirm your faith in the afterlife

3

رَبَّنَا مَا خَلَقْتَ هَٰذَا بَاطِلًا سُبْحَانَكَ فَقِنَا عَذَابَ ٱلنَّارِ

Rabbanaa maa khalaqta haaza baatilan Subhaanaka faqinaa 'azaaban Naar

"Our Lord, You did not create this aimlessly; exalted are You [above such a thing]; then protect us from the punishment of the Fire."

Qur'an 3:191

A dua'a asking Allah (swt) for protection from hell

4

رَبَّنَآ إِنَّكَ مَن تُدْخِلِ ٱلنَّارَ فَقَدْ أَخْزَيْتَهُۥ وَمَا لِلظَّٰلِمِينَ مِنْ أَنصَارٍ

Rabbanaaa innaka man tudkhilin Naara faqad akhzai tahoo wa maa lizzaalimeena min ansaar

"Our Lord, indeed whoever You admit to the Fire – You have disgraced him, and for the wrongdoers there are no helpers."

Qur'an 3:192

A dua'a to remind yourself of the afterlife

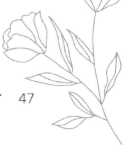

47

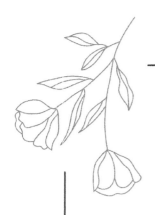

5

رَبَّنَا وَءَاتِنَا مَا وَعَدتَّنَا عَلَىٰ رُسُلِكَ وَلَا تُخْزِنَا يَوْمَ ٱلْقِيَٰمَةِ ۗ إِنَّكَ لَا تُخْلِفُ ٱلْمِيعَادَ

Rabbanaa wa aatinaa maa wa'attanaa 'alaa Rusulika wa laa tukhzinaa Yawmal Qiyaamah; innaka laa tukhliful mee'aad

"Our Lord, and grant us what You promised us through Your messengers and do not disgrace us on the Day of Resurrection. Indeed, You do not fail in [Your] promise."

Qur'an 3:194

A dua'a of humility and protection from being disgraced on the day of judgement

6

وَٱكْتُبْ لَنَا فِى هَٰذِهِ ٱلدُّنْيَا حَسَنَةً وَفِى ٱلْآخِرَةِ إِنَّا هُدْنَآ إِلَيْكَ

Waktub lanaa fee haazi hid dunyaa hasanatanw wa fil Aakhirati innaa hudnaaa ilaik

"And decree for us in this world [that which is] good and [also] in the Hereafter; indeed, we have turned back to You."

Qur'an 7:156

A dua'a asking Allah (swt) for success in this life and the hereafter

7

رَبَّنَا أَصْرِفْ عَنَّا عَذَابَ جَهَنَّمَ ۖ إِنَّ عَذَابَهَا كَانَ غَرَامًا ۖ إِنَّهَا سَاءَتْ مُسْتَقَرًّا وَمُقَامًا

*Rabbanas rif 'annnaa 'azaaba Jahannama
inn 'azaabahaa kaana gharaamaa Innahaa
saaa'at mustaqarranw wa muqaamaa*

"Our Lord, avert from us the punishment of
Hell. Indeed, its punishment is ever adhering;
Indeed, it is evil as a settlement and
residence."

Qur'an 25:65-66

A du'a to remind yourself of hell and asking
for protection from it

8

وَٱجۡعَلۡنِی مِن وَرَثَةِ جَنَّةِ ٱلنَّعِيمِ

*Waj'alnee minw warasati Jannnatin
Na'eem*

"And place me among the inheritors
of the Garden of Pleasure."

Qur'an 26:85

A du'a asking Allah (swt) for a place
in Jannah

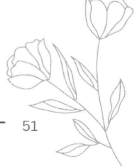

9

 وَلَا تُخْزِنِى يَوْمَ يُبْعَثُونَ

Wa laa tukhzinee Yawma yub'asoon

"And do not disgrace me on the Day
they are [all] resurrected."

Qur'an 26:87

A du'a asking Allah (swt) for
protection on the day of judgement

10

رَبَّنَا لَغَفُورٌ شَكُورٌ

Rabbana la Ghafurun shakur

"Our Lord is Forgiving and Appreciative."

Qur'an 35:34

A du'a that will be recited by the believers when they enter the Garden of Eden

11

رَبَّنَا وَأَدْخِلْهُمْ جَنَّتِ عَدْنٍ ٱلَّتِي وَعَدتَّهُمْ وَمَن صَلَحَ مِنْ ءَابَآ بِهِمْ وَأَزْوَٰجِهِمْ وَذُرِّيَّتِهِمْ إِنَّكَ أَنتَ ٱلْعَزِيزُ ٱلْحَكِيمُ وَقِهِمُ ٱلسَّيِّعَاتِ وَمَن تَقِ ٱلسَّيِّعَاتِ يَوْمَئِذٍ فَقَدْ رَحِمْتَهُ وَذَٰلِكَ هُوَ ٱلْفَوْزُ ٱلْعَظِيمُ

Rabbana wa adhkhilhum Jannati 'adninil-lati wa'attahum wa man salaha min aba'ihim wa azwajihim wa dhuriyyatihim innaka antal 'Azizul-Hakim Waqihimus saiyi'at wa man taqis-saiyi'ati yawma'idhin faqad rahimatahu wa dhalika huwal fawzul-'Adheem

"Our Lord, and admit them to gardens of perpetual residence which You have promised them and whoever was righteous among their forefathers, their spouses and their offspring. Indeed, it is You who is the Exalted in Might, the Wise. And protect them from the evil consequences [of their deeds]. And he whom You protect from evil consequences that Day - You will have given him mercy. And that is the great attainment."

Qur'an 40:8-9

A du'a asking Allah (swt) to unite the believers with their descendants in Jannah and for protection and mercy on the day of judgement

12

رَّبَّنَا ٱكْشِفْ عَنَّا ٱلْعَذَابَ إِنَّا مُؤْمِنُونَ

Rabbanak shif 'annal 'azaaba innaa mu'minoon

"Our Lord, remove from us the torment; indeed, we are believers."

Qur'an 44:12

A du'a asking Allah (swt) for protection from the hell-fire

13

رَبَّنَآ أَتْمِمْ لَنَا نُورَنَا وَاغْفِرْ لَنَآ إِنَّكَ عَلَىٰ كُلِّ شَيْءٍ قَدِيرٌ

*Rabbanaaa atmim lanaa nooranaa
waghfir lana innaka 'alaa kulli shai'in
qadeer*

"Our Lord, perfect for us our light and
forgive us. Indeed, You are over all things
competent."

Qur'an 66:8

A du'a asking for Jannah and forgiveness

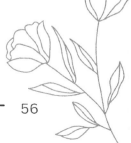

14

رَبِّ ٱبْنِ لِى عِندَكَ بَيْتًا فِى ٱلْجَنَّةِ وَنَجِّنِى مِن فِرْعَوْنَ وَعَمَلِهِۦ وَنَجِّنِى مِنَ ٱلْقَوْمِ ٱلظَّٰلِمِينَ

Rab bibni lee 'indaka baitan fil jannati wa najjinee min Fir'awna wa 'amalihee wa najjinee minal qawmiz zaalimeen

"My Lord, build for me near You a house in Paradise and save me from Pharaoh and his deeds and save me from the wrongdoing people."

Qur'an 66:11

A du'a asking for Allah (swt) to grant us a place in Jannah

Asking Allah for good in this world

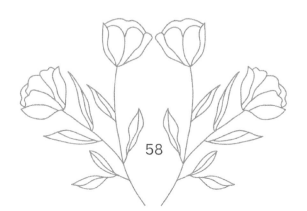

1

رَبَّنَآ ءَاتِنَا فِى ٱلدُّنْيَا حَسَنَةً وَفِى ٱلْآخِرَةِ حَسَنَةً وَقِنَا عَذَابَ ٱلنَّارِ

Rabbana atina fid dunyaa hasanatanw wa fil aakhirati hasanatanw wa qinaa azaaban Naar

"Our Lord, give us in this world [that which is] good and in the Hereafter [that which is] good and protect us from the punishment of the Fire."

Qur'an 2:201

A du'a asking for Allah (swt) to grant you good in this world but also the Akhira

59

2

رَبَّنَآ أَفۡرِغۡ عَلَيۡنَا صَبۡرٗا وَثَبِّتۡ أَقۡدَامَنَا وَٱنصُرۡنَا عَلَى ٱلۡقَوۡمِ ٱلۡكَٰفِرِينَ

Rabbana afrigh 'alainaa sabranw wa sabbit aqdaamanaa wansurnaa 'alal qawmil kaafireen

"Our Lord, pour upon us patience and plant firmly our feet and give us victory over the disbelieving people."

Qur'an 2:250

A du'a asking Allah (swt) for protection, patience in your endeavours and to be victorious

3

رَبَّنَا وَلَا تُحَمِّلْنَا مَا لَا طَاقَةَ لَنَا بِهِ ۖ وَٱعْفُ عَنَّا وَٱغْفِرْ لَنَا وَٱرْحَمْنَا ۚ أَنتَ مَوْلَىٰنَا فَٱنصُرْنَا عَلَى ٱلْقَوْمِ ٱلْكَٰفِرِينَ

Rabbana wa laa tuhammilnaa maa laa taaqata lanaa bih; wa'fu 'annaa waghfir lanaa warhamnaa; Anta mawlaanaa fansurnaa 'alal qawmil kaafireen

"Our Lord, and burden us not with that which we have no ability to bear. And pardon us; and forgive us; and have mercy upon us. You are our protector, so give us victory over the disbelieving people."

Qur'an 2:286

Three powerful dua's, if memorised at night, will be sufficient for you

4

رَبَّنَا ٱغْفِرْ لَنَا ذُنُوبَنَا وَإِسْرَافَنَا فِي أَمْرِنَا وَثَبِّتْ أَقْدَامَنَا وَٱنصُرْنَا عَلَى ٱلْقَوْمِ ٱلْكَٰفِرِينَ

Rabbanagh fir lanaa zunoobanaa wa israafanaa feee amrinaa wa sabbit aqdaamanaa wansurnaa 'alal qawmil kaafireen

"Our Lord, forgive us our sins and the excess [committed] in our affairs and plant firmly our feet and give us victory over the disbelieving people."

Qur'an 3:147

A dua'a asking Allah (swt) for forgiveness, victory and resiliency

Success

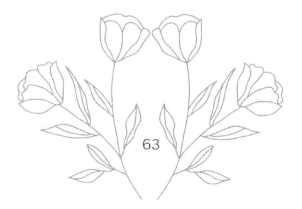

1

وَٱكْتُبْ لَنَا فِى هَٰذِهِ ٱلدُّنْيَا حَسَنَةً وَفِى ٱلْآخِرَةِ إِنَّا هُدْنَآ إِلَيْكَ

*Waktub lanaa fee haazi hid dunyaa
hasanatanw wa fil Aakhirati innaa
hudnaaa ilaik*

"And decree for us in this world [that
which is] good and [also] in the
Hereafter; indeed, we have turned back
to You."

Qur'an 7:156

A dua'a asking Allah (swt) for success in
this life and the hereafter

2

رَبَّنَا لَا تَجْعَلْنَا فِتْنَةً لِّلَّذِينَ كَفَرُوا وَٱغْفِرْ لَنَا رَبَّنَآ إِنَّكَ أَنتَ ٱلْعَزِيزُ ٱلْحَكِيمُ

Rabbana laa taj'alnaa fitnatal lillazeena kafaroo waghfir lanaa rabbanaaa innaka antal azeezul hakeem

"Our Lord, make us not [objects of] torment for the disbelievers and forgive us, our Lord. Indeed, it is You who is the Exalted in Might, the Wise."

Qur'an 60:5

A du'a asking Allah (swt) to make the believers victorious over the disbelievers

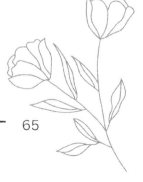

Patience

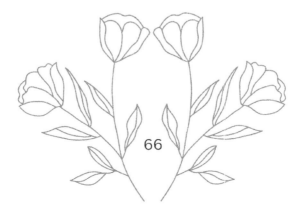

1

يَـٰٓأَيُّهَا ٱلَّذِينَ ءَامَنُوا۟ ٱسْتَعِينُوا۟ بِٱلصَّبْرِ وَٱلصَّلَوٰةِ ۚ إِنَّ ٱللَّهَ مَعَ ٱلصَّـٰبِرِينَ

Yaaa ayyuhal laazeena aamanus ta'eenoo bissabri was Salaah; innal laaha ma'as-saabireen

"O you who have believed, seek help through patience and prayer. Indeed, Allah is with the patient."

Qur'an 2:153

A du'a asking Allah (swt) for patience

2

رَبَّنَآ أَفْرِغْ عَلَيْنَا صَبْرًا وَثَبِّتْ أَقْدَامَنَا وَأَنصُرْنَا عَلَى ٱلْقَوْمِ ٱلْكَٰفِرِينَ

*Rabbana afrigh 'alainaa sabranw wa sabbit
aqdaamanaa wansurnaa 'alal qawmil
kaafireen*

"Our Lord, pour upon us patience and plant
firmly our feet and give us victory over the
disbelieving people."

Qur'an 2:250

A du'a asking Allah (swt) for protection,
patience in your endeavours and to be
victorious

3

رَبَّنَآ أَفْرِغْ عَلَيْنَا صَبْرًا وَتَوَفَّنَا مُسْلِمِينَ

*Rabbanaaa afrigh 'alainaa sabranw
wa tawaffanaa muslimeen*

"Our Lord, pour upon us patience and
let us die as Muslims [in submission to
You]."

Qur'an 7:126

A dua'a asking Allah (swt) for sabr,
perseverance, and a righteous death

4

رَبَّنَآ ءَاتِنَا مِن لَّدُنكَ رَحْمَةً وَهَيِّئ لَنَا مِنْ أَمْرِنَا رَشَدًا

Rabbanaaa aatinaa mil ladunka
rahmatanw wa haiyi' lanaa min
amrinaa rashadaa

"Our Lord, grant us from Yourself mercy
and prepare for us from our affair right
guidance."

Qur'an 18:10

A dua'a asking for Allah's (swt)
approval, mercy, provision and
patience

Protection

1

رَبَّنَآ أَفۡرِغۡ عَلَيۡنَا صَبۡرًا وَثَبِّتۡ أَقۡدَامَنَا وَٱنصُرۡنَا عَلَى ٱلۡقَوۡمِ ٱلۡكَٰفِرِينَ

Rabbana afrigh 'alainaa sabranw wa sabbit aqdaamanaa wansurnaa 'alal qawmil kaafireen

"Our Lord, pour upon us patience and plant firmly our feet and give us victory over the disbelieving people."

Qur'an 2:250

A du'a asking Allah (swt) for protection, patience in your endeavours and to be victorious

2

رَبَّنَآ إِنَّنَآ ءَامَنَّا فَٱغْفِرْ لَنَا ذُنُوبَنَا وَقِنَا عَذَابَ ٱلنَّارِ

Rabbanaaa innanaaa aamannaa faghfir lanaa zunoobanaa wa qinaa 'azaaban Naar

"Our Lord, indeed we have believed, so forgive us our sins and protect us from the punishment of the Fire"

Qur'an 3:16

A dua'a for repentance and protection

3

رَبَّنَآ أَخْرِجْنَا مِنْ هَـٰذِهِ ٱلْقَرْيَةِ ٱلظَّالِمِ أَهْلُهَا وَٱجْعَل لَّنَا مِن لَّدُنكَ وَلِيًّا وَٱجْعَل لَّنَا مِن لَّدُنكَ نَصِيرًا

Rabbanaaa akhrijnaa min haazihil qaryatiz zaalimi ahluhaa waj'al lanaa mil ladunka waliyanw waj'al lanaa mil ladunka naseeraa

"Our Lord! cause us to go forth from this town, whose people are oppressors, and give us from Thee a guardian and give us from Thee a helper."

Qur'an 4:75

A du'a asking Allah (swt) for protection

4

رَبَّنَا لَا تَجْعَلْنَا مَعَ ٱلْقَوْمِ ٱلظَّٰلِمِينَ

Rabbanaa laa taj'alnaa ma'al qawmiz zaalimeen

"Our Lord, do not place us with the wrongdoing people."

Qur'an 7:47

A dua'a asking Allah (swt) to protect us from associating with the wrong people

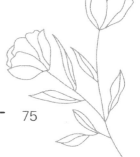

5

وَإِن تَوَلَّوْا۟ فَٱعْلَمُوٓا۟ أَنَّ ٱللَّهَ مَوْلَىٰكُمْ ۚ نِعْمَ ٱلْمَوْلَىٰ وَنِعْمَ
ٱلنَّصِيرُ

*Wa in tawallaw fa'lamooo annal
laaha mawlaakum; ni'mal mawlaa
wa ni'man naseer*

"But if they refuse, be sure that Allah
is your Protector - the best to
protect and the best to help."

Qur'an 8:40

A dua'a asking Allah (swt) for
protection

6

لَّن يُصِيبَنَآ إِلَّا مَا كَتَبَ ٱللَّهُ لَنَا هُوَ مَوْلَٰنَا

Lany-yuseebanaaa illaa maa katabal laahu lanaa Huwa mawlaanaa

"Never will we be struck except by what Allah has decreed for us; He is our protector."

Qur'an 9:51

A dua'a for safety

7

عَلَى ٱللَّهِ تَوَكَّلْنَا رَبَّنَا لَا تَجْعَلْنَا فِتْنَةً لِلْقَوْمِ ٱلظَّالِمِينَ وَنَجِّنَا بِرَحْمَتِكَ مِنَ ٱلْقَوْمِ ٱلْكَافِرِينَ

Al laahi tawakkalnaa Rabbanaa laa taj'alnaa fitnatal lilqawmiz zaalimeen Wa najjinaa birahmatika minal qawmil kaafireen

"Upon Allah do we rely. Our Lord, make us not [objects of] trial for the wrongdoing people And save us by Your mercy from the disbelieving people."

Qur'an 10:85-86

A dua'a asking Allah (swt) for protection from evil and unjust people

8

يَعْلَمُ مَا بَيْنَ أَيْدِيهِمْ وَمَا خَلْفَهُمْ وَلَا يَشْفَعُونَ إِلَّا لِمَنِ ارْتَضَى وَهُم مِّنْ خَشْيَتِهِ مُشْفِقُونَ

Ya'lamu maa baina aideehim wa maa khalfahum wa laa yashfa'oona illaa limanir tadaa wa hum min khash yatihee mushfiqoon

"He knows what is [presently] before them and what will be after them, and they cannot intercede except on behalf of one whom He approves. And they, from fear of Him, are apprehensive."

Qur'an 21:28

A dua'a for protection from the enemy during war or adversity

9

ٱلْحَمْدُ لِلَّهِ ٱلَّذِى نَجَّىٰنَا مِنَ ٱلْقَوْمِ ٱلظَّٰلِمِينَ وَقُل رَّبِّ أَنزِلْنِى مُنزَلًا مُّبَارَكًا وَأَنتَ خَيْرُ ٱلْمُنزِلِينَ

Alhamdu lillaahil lazee najjaanaa minal qawmiz zalimeen. Wa qur Rabbi anzilnee munzalam mubaarakanw wa Anta khairul munzileen

"All praise belongs to Allah, who has delivered us from the wrongdoing lot." And say, "My Lord! Land me with a blessed landing, for You are the best of those who bring ashore."

Qur'an 23:28-29

A du'a asking for Allah's (swt) protection from the oppressors

10

رَبِّ ٱنصُرْنِى بِمَا كَذَّبُونِ

Rabbin surnee bimaa kazzaboon

"O my Lord! help me: for that they accuse me of falsehood."

Qur'an 23:39

A du'a asking for Allah's (swt) protection from the oppressors

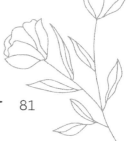

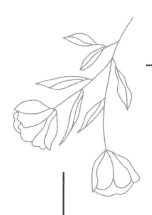

11

رَّبِّ أَعُوذُ بِكَ مِنْ هَمَزَٰتِ ٱلشَّيَٰطِينِ وَأَعُوذُ بِكَ رَبِّ أَن يَحْضُرُونِ

Rabbi a'oozu bika min hamazaatish Shayaateen Wa a'oozu bika Rabbi ai-yahduroon

"My Lord, I seek refuge in You from the incitements of the devils, And I seek refuge in You, my Lord, lest they be present with me."

Qur'an 23:97-98

A du'a asking for Allah's (swt) protection from the evildoers

12

رَبِّ نَجِّنِى وَأَهۡلِى مِمَّا يَعۡمَلُونَ

Rabbi najjjinee wa ahlee mimmmaa ya'maloon

"My Lord! Save me and my family from what they do."

Qur'an 26:169

A du'a asking Allah (swt) for protection

13

رَبِّ نَجِّنِى مِنَ ٱلْقَوْمِ ٱلظَّٰلِمِينَ

Rabbi najjinee minal qawmiz zaalimeen

"My Lord, save me from the wrongdoing people."

Qur'an 28:21

A du'a asking Allah (swt) for protection from evildoers

14

رَبِّ ٱنصُرْنِى عَلَى ٱلْقَوْمِ ٱلْمُفْسِدِينَ

Rabbin surnee 'alal qawmil mufsideen

"My Lord, support me against the corrupting people."

Qur'an 29:30

A du'a asking Allah (swt) for protection from evildoers

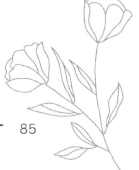

Forgiveness

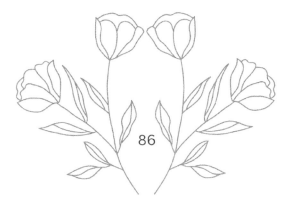

1

سَمِعْنَا وَأَطَعْنَا ۚ غُفْرَانَكَ رَبَّنَا وَإِلَيْكَ ٱلْمَصِيرُ

*Sami'naa wa ata'naa ghufraanaka
Rabbanaa wa ilaikal-maseer*

"We hear and obey, our Lord, grant
us Thy forgiveness and to Thee is the
end of all journeys."

Qur'an 2:285

A du'a asking Allah (swt) for
forgiveness

2

رَبَّنَا لَا تُؤَاخِذْنَآ إِن نَّسِينَآ أَوْ أَخْطَأْنَا

Rabbana laa tu'aakhiznaaa in naseenaaa aw akhtaanaa

"Our Lord, do not impose blame upon us if we have forgotten or erred."

Qur'an 2:286

A du'a asking Allah (swt) for forgiveness

3

رَبَّنَاۤ إِنَّنَاۤ ءَامَنَّا فَٱغۡفِرۡ لَنَا ذُنُوبَنَا وَقِنَا عَذَابَ ٱلنَّارِ

Rabbanaaa innanaaa aamannaa faghfir lanaa zunoobanaa wa qinaa 'azaaban Naar

"Our Lord, indeed we have believed, so forgive us our sins and protect us from the punishment of the Fire."

Qur'an 3:16

A dua'a for repentance and protection

4

رَبَّنَا أغْفِرْ لَنَا ذُنُوبَنَا وَإِسْرَافَنَا فِي أَمْرِنَا وَثَبِّتْ أَقْدَامَنَا وَانصُرْنَا عَلَى ٱلْقَوْمِ ٱلْكَٰفِرِينَ

*Rabbanagh fir lanaa zunoobanaa wa
israafanaa feee amrinaa wa sabbit
aqdaamanaa wansurnaa 'alal qawmil
kaafireen*

"Our Lord, forgive us our sins and the
excess [committed] in our affairs and
plant firmly our feet and give us victory
over the disbelieving people."

Qur'an 3:147

A dua'a asking Allah (swt) for
forgiveness, victory and resiliency

5

رَبَّنَا فَٱغْفِرْ لَنَا ذُنُوبَنَا وَكَفِّرْ عَنَّا سَيِّئَاتِنَا وَتَوَفَّنَا مَعَ ٱلْأَبْرَارِ

*Rabbanaa faghfir lanaa zunoobanaa
wa kaffir 'annaa saiyi aatina wa
tawaffanaa ma'al abraar*

"Our Lord, so forgive us our sins and
remove from us our misdeeds and
cause us to die among the righteous."

Qur'an 3:193

A dua'a for repentance and asking
Allah (swt) to take us while we are
guided on the right path

6

رَبَّنَا ظَلَمْنَا أَنفُسَنَا وَإِن لَّمْ تَغْفِرْ لَنَا وَتَرْحَمْنَا لَنَكُونَنَّ مِنَ الْخَاسِرِينَ

Rabbanaa zalamnaaa anfusanaa wa illam taghfir lanaa wa tarhamnaa lanakoonanna minal khaasireen

"Our Lord, we have wronged ourselves, and if You do not forgive us and have mercy upon us, we will surely be among the losers."

Qur'an 7:23

A dua'a asking for forgiveness

92

7

رَبِّ ٱغْفِرْ لِى وَلِأَخِى وَأَدْخِلْنَا فِى رَحْمَتِكَ ۖ وَأَنتَ أَرْحَمُ ٱلرَّٰحِمِينَ

Rabbighfirlee wa li akhee wa adkhilnaa fee rahmatika wa Anta arhamur raahimeen

"My Lord, forgive me and my brother and admit us into Your mercy, for You are the most merciful of the merciful."

Qur'an 7:151

A dua'a for believers

8

أَنتَ وَلِيُّنَا فَٱغْفِرْ لَنَا وَٱرْحَمْنَا ۖ وَأَنتَ خَيْرُ ٱلْغَـٰفِرِينَ

Anta waliyyunaa faghfir lanaa warhamnaa wa Anta khairul ghaafireen

"You are our Protector, so forgive us and have mercy upon us; and You are the best of forgivers."

Qur'an 7:155

A dua'a asking Allah (swt) for forgiveness

9

سَلَمٌ عَلَيْكَ سَأَسْتَغْفِرُ لَكَ رَبِّیَ ۖ إِنَّهُ كَانَ بِی حَفِیًّا

*Salaamun 'alaika sa astaghfiru laka
Rabbeee innahoo kaana bee
hafiyyaa*

"Peace will be upon you. I will ask
forgiveness for you of my Lord.
Indeed, He is ever gracious to me."

Qur'an 19:47

A dua'a to help forgive

10

رَّبِّ إِمَّا تُرِيَنِّى مَا يُوعَدُونَ رَبِّ فَلَا تَجْعَلْنِى فِى ٱلْقَوْمِ ٱلظَّٰلِمِينَ

Rabbi immmaa turiyannee maa yoo'adoon Rabbi falaa taj'alnee fil qawmiz zaalimeen

"My Lord, if You should show me that which they are promised, My Lord, then do not place me among the wrongdoing people."

Qur'an 23:93-94

A du'a for attaining salvation of forgiveness

11

رَبَّنَاۤ ءَامَنَّا فَٱغۡفِرۡ لَنَا وَٱرۡحَمۡنَا وَأَنتَ خَيۡرُ ٱلرَّٰحِمِينَ

Rabbanaaa aamannaa faghfir lanaa warhamnaa wa Anta khairur raahimeen

"Our Lord we believe; therefore forgive us and have mercy on us, for thou art the best of the Merciful."

Qur'an 23:109

A du'a for forgiveness

97

12

رَّبِّ ٱغْفِرْ وَٱرْحَمْ وَأَنتَ خَيْرُ ٱلرَّاحِمِينَ

Rabbigh fir warham wa Anta khairur raahimeen

"My Lord, forgive and have mercy, and You are the best of the merciful."

Qur'an 23:118

A du'a asking for Allah's (swt) forgiveness

13

إِنَّا نَطْمَعُ أَن يَغْفِرَ لَنَا رَبُّنَا خَطَايَانَا أَن كُنَّا أَوَّلَ ٱلْمُؤْمِنِينَ

*Innaa natma'u ai yaghfira lanaa
Rabbunaa khataa yaanaaa an kunnaaa
awwalal mu'mineen*

"Indeed, we aspire that our Lord will
forgive us our sins because we were the
first of the believers."

Qur'an 26:51

A du'a asking for attaining salvation of
forgiveness

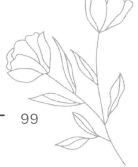

14

رَبِّ إِنِّى ظَلَمْتُ نَفْسِى فَٱغْفِرْ لِى

Rabbi innee zalamtu nafsee faghfir lee

"My Lord, indeed I have wronged myself, so forgive me."

Qur'an 28:16

A du'a asking Allah (swt) for forgiveness

15

يَغْفِرُ لِمَن يَشَاءُ وَيُعَذِّبُ مَن يَشَاءُ ۚ وَكَانَ ٱللَّهُ غَفُورًا رَّحِيمًا

*Yaghfiru limany yashaaa'u wa yu'azzibu
many yashaaa'; wa kaanal laahu
Ghafoorar Raheemaa*

"He forgives whom He wills and punishes
whom He wills. And ever is Allah Forgiving
and Merciful."

Qur'an 48:14

A du'a for forgiveness

16

رَبَّنَا ٱغْفِرْ لَنَا وَ لِإِخْوَٰنِنَا ٱلَّذِينَ سَبَقُونَا بِٱلْإِيمَٰنِ وَ لَا تَجْعَلْ فِى قُلُوبِنَا غِلًّا لِّلَّذِينَ ءَامَنُوا۟

Rabbanagh fir lanaa wa li ikhwaani nal lazeena sabqoonaa bil eemaani wa laa taj'al fee quloobinaa ghillalil lazeena aamanoo

"Our Lord, forgive us and our brothers who preceded us in faith and put not in our hearts [any] resentment toward those who have believed."

Qur'an 59:10

A du'a asking for forgiveness for fellow Muslims and for no resentment towards one another

17

رَبَّنَآ أَتْمِمْ لَنَا نُورَنَا وَاغْفِرْ لَنَآ إِنَّكَ عَلَىٰ كُلِّ شَيْءٍ قَدِيرٌ

*Rabbanaaa atmim lanaa nooranaa waghfir
lana innaka 'alaa kulli shai'in qadeer*

"Our Lord, perfect for us our light and forgive
us. Indeed, You are over all things
competent."

Qur'an 66:8

A du'a asking for Jannah and forgiveness

18

رَّبِّ ٱغْفِرْ لِى وَلِوَٰلِدَىَّ وَلِمَن دَخَلَ بَيْتِىَ مُؤْمِنًا وَلِلْمُؤْمِنِينَ وَٱلْمُؤْمِنَـٰتِ وَلَا تَزِدِ ٱلظَّـٰلِمِينَ إِلَّا تَبَارًۢا

Rabbigh fir lee wa liwaa lidaiya wa liman dakhala baitiya mu'minanw wa lil mu'mineena wal mu'minaati wa laa tazidiz zaalimeena illaa tabaaraa

"My Lord, forgive me and my parents and whoever enters my house a believer and the believing men and believing women. And do not increase the wrongdoers except in destruction."

Qur'an 71:28

A du'a asking for Allah (swt) to forgive our parents

Mercy

1

رَبَّنَا لَا تُزِغْ قُلُوبَنَا بَعْدَ إِذْ هَدَيْتَنَا وَهَبْ لَنَا مِن لَّدُنكَ رَحْمَةً إِنَّكَ أَنتَ ٱلْوَهَّابُ

Rabbana laa tuzigh quloobanaa ba'da iz hadaitanaa wa hab lanaa mil ladunka rahmah; innaka antal Wahhaab

"Our Lord, let not our hearts deviate after You have guided us and grant us from Yourself mercy. Indeed, You are the Bestower."

Qur'an 3:8

A dua'a asking for Allah's mercy

2

رَبِّ ٱغْفِرْ لِى وَلِأَخِى وَأَدْخِلْنَا فِى رَحْمَتِكَ ۖ وَأَنتَ أَرْحَمُ
ٱلرَّٰحِمِينَ

*Rabbighfirlee wa li akhee wa
adkhilnaa fee rahmatika wa Anta
arhamur raahimeen*

"My Lord, forgive me and my brother
and admit us into Your mercy, for
You are the most merciful of the
merciful."

Qur'an 7:151

A dua'a for believers

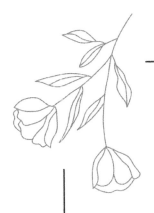

3

رَبَّنَآ ءَاتِنَا مِن لَّدُنكَ رَحْمَةً وَهَيِّئْ لَنَا مِنْ أَمْرِنَا رَشَدًا

Rabbanaaa aatinaa mil ladunka rahmatanw wa haiyi' lanaa min amrinaa rashadaa

"Our Lord, grant us from Yourself mercy and prepare for us from our affair right guidance."

Qur'an 18:10

A dua'a asking for Allah's (swt) approval, mercy, provision and patience

4

رَبَّنَآ ءَامَنَّا فَٱغْفِرْ لَنَا وَٱرْحَمْنَا وَأَنتَ خَيْرُ ٱلرَّٰحِمِينَ

*Rabbanaaa aamannaa faghfir lanaa
warhamnaa wa Anta khairur raahimeen*

"Our Lord, we have believed, so forgive us
and have mercy upon us, and You are the
best of the merciful."

Qur'an 23:109

A du'a asking for Allah's (swt) mercy and
calling upon by his rightful attribute of
being Ar-Rahim

5

رَبَّنَا وَسِعْتَ كُلَّ شَىْءٍ رَّحْمَةً وَعِلْمًا فَٱغْفِرْ لِلَّذِينَ تَابُوا۟ وَٱتَّبَعُوا۟ سَبِيلَكَ وَقِهِمْ عَذَابَ ٱلْجَحِيمِ

*Rabbanaa wasi'ta kulla shai'ir rahmatanw
wa 'ilman faghfir lillazeena taaboo
wattaba'oo sabeelaka wa qihim 'azaabal
Jaheem*

"Our Lord, You have encompassed all
things in mercy and knowledge, so forgive
those who have repented and followed
Your way and protect them from the
punishment of Hellfire."

Qur'an 40:7

A du'a asking Allah (swt) to be merciful
towards all those who believe and have
sought repentance

6

رَبَّنَا وَأَدْخِلْهُمْ جَنَّـٰتِ عَدْنٍ ٱلَّتِى وَعَدتَّهُمْ وَمَن صَلَحَ مِنْ ءَابَآئِهِمْ وَأَزْوَٰجِهِمْ وَذُرِّيَّـٰتِهِمْ إِنَّكَ أَنتَ ٱلْعَزِيزُ ٱلْحَكِيمُ وَقِهِمُ ٱلسَّيِّـَٔاتِ وَمَن تَقِ ٱلسَّيِّـَٔاتِ يَوْمَئِذٍ فَقَدْ رَحِمْتَهُ وَذَٰلِكَ هُوَ ٱلْفَوْزُ ٱلْعَظِيمُ

Rabbana wa adhkhilhum Jannati 'adninil-lati wa'attahum wa man salaha min aba'ihim wa azwajihim wa dhuriyyatihim innaka antal 'Azizul-Hakim, waqihimus saiyi'at wa man taqis-saiyi'ati yawma'idhin faqad rahimatahu wa dhalika huwal fawzul-'Adheem

"Our Lord, and admit them to gardens of perpetual residence which You have promised them and whoever was righteous among their forefathers, their spouses and their offspring. Indeed, it is You who is the Exalted in Might, the Wise. And protect them from the evil consequences [of their deeds]. And he whom You protect from evil consequences that Day – You will have given him mercy. And that is the great attainment."

Qur'an 40:8-9

A du'a asking Allah (swt) to unite the believers with their descendants in Jannah and for protection and mercy on the day of judgement

7

سُبْحَٰنَ رَبِّنَآ إِنَّا كُنَّا ظَٰلِمِينَ

Subhaana rabbinaaa innaa kunnaa zaalimeen

"Exalted is our Lord! Indeed, we were wrongdoers."

Qur'an 68:29

A du'a asking for Allah (swt) to show His mercy and remove difficulties

Provision

1

اللَّهُمَّ رَبَّنَا أَنزِلْ عَلَيْنَا مَآئِدَةً مِّنَ ٱلسَّمَآءِ تَكُونُ لَنَا عِيدًا لِّأَوَّلِنَا وَءَاخِرِنَا وَءَايَةً مِّنكَ وَٱرْزُقْنَا وَأَنتَ خَيْرُ ٱلرَّٰزِقِينَ

Rabbanaaa anzil 'alainaa maaa'idatam minas samaaa'i takoonu lanaa 'eedal li awwalinaa wa aakhirinaa wa Aayatam minka warzuqnaa wa Anta khairur raaziqeen

"O Allah, our Lord, send down to us a table [spread with food] from the heaven to be for us a festival for the first of us and the last of us and a sign from You. And provide for us, and You are the best of providers."

Qur'an 5:114

A dua'a asking for provision

2

رَبَّنَآ ءَاتِنَا مِن لَّدُنكَ رَحْمَةً وَهَيِّئْ لَنَا مِنْ أَمْرِنَا رَشَدًا

*Rabbanaaa aatinaa mil ladunka
rahmatanw wa haiyi' lanaa min
amrinaa rashadaa*

"Our Lord, grant us from Yourself mercy
and prepare for us from our affair right
guidance."

Qur'an 18:10

A dua'a asking for Allah's (swt)
approval, mercy, provision and
patience

3

وَفَعَلْتَ فَعْلَتَكَ ٱلَّتِى فَعَلْتَ وَأَنتَ مِنَ ٱلْكَـٰفِرِينَ

Wa fa'alta fa'latakal latee fa'alta wa anta minal kaafireen

"And [then] you did your deed which you did, and you were of the ungrateful."

Qur'an 26:19

A du'a asking for wealth and prosperity

4

إِنَّ ٱللَّهَ هُوَ ٱلرَّزَّاقُ ذُو ٱلْقُوَّةِ ٱلْمَتِينُ

*Innal laaha Huwar Razzaaqu Zul
Quwwatil Mateen*

"Indeed, it is Allah who is the
[continual] Provider, the firm
possessor of strength."

Qur'an 51:58

A du'a asking Allah (swt) for wealth
and prosperity

5

وَيَرْزُقْهُ مِنْ حَيْثُ لَا يَحْتَسِبُ وَمَن يَتَوَكَّلْ عَلَى ٱللَّهِ فَهُوَ حَسْبُهُۥ إِنَّ ٱللَّهَ بَٰلِغُ أَمْرِهِۦ قَدْ جَعَلَ ٱللَّهُ لِكُلِّ شَىْءٍ قَدْرًا

Wa yarzuqhu min haisu laa yahtasib; wa many yatawakkal 'alal laahi fahuwa hasbuh; innal laaha baalighu amrih; qad ja'alal laahu likulli shai'in qadraa

"And provide for him from whence he does not count upon. And whoever puts his trust in Allah, He will suffice him. Indeed Allah carries through His commands. Certainly, Allah has ordained a measure [and extent] for everything."

Qur'an 65:3

A du'a asking Allah (swt) for sustenance

Hardships

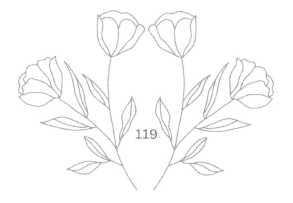

1

أُوْلَـٰٓئِكَ ٱلَّذِينَ ٱشۡتَرَوُاْ ٱلۡحَيَوٰةَ ٱلدُّنۡيَا بِٱلۡأٓخِرَةِ ۖ فَلَا يُخَفَّفُ عَنۡهُمُ ٱلۡعَذَابُ وَلَا هُمۡ يُنصَرُونَ

Ulaaa'ikal lazeenash tarawul hayaatad dunyaa bil aakhirati falaa yukhaffafu 'anhumul 'azaabu wa laa hum yunsaroon

"Those are the ones who have bought the life of this world [in exchange] for the Hereafter, so the punishment will not be lightened for them, nor will they be aided."

Qur'an 2:86

A du'a to recite while facing hardship

2

مَن يُنَجِّيكُم مِّن ظُلُمَـٰتِ ٱلْبَرِّ وَٱلْبَحْرِ تَدْعُونَهُۥ تَضَرُّعًا وَخُفْيَةً لَّئِنْ أَنجَىٰنَا مِنْ هَـٰذِهِۦ لَنَكُونَنَّ مِنَ ٱلشَّـٰكِرِينَ

Mai yunajjeekum min zulumaatil barri walbahri tad'oonahoo tadarru'anw wa khufyatal la'in anjaanaa min haazihee lanakoonanna minash shaakireen

"Who rescues you from the darknesses of the land and sea [when] you call upon Him imploring [aloud] and privately, 'If He should save us from this [crisis], we will surely be among the thankful.'"

Qur'an 6:63

A dua'a asking Allah (swt) to alleviate suffering

3

رَبِّ اشْرَحْ لِى صَدْرِى وَيَسِّرْ لِى أَمْرِى

Rabbish rah lee sadree Wa yassir leee amree

"My Lord, expand for me my breast [with assurance]And ease for me my task."

Qur'an 20:25-26

A dua'a asking for Allah's (swt) help and assistance

4

رَبِّ ٱشْرَحْ لِى صَدْرِى وَيَسِّرْ لِىٓ أَمْرِى وَٱحْلُلْ عُقْدَةً مِّن لِّسَانِى يَفْقَهُوا۟ قَوْلِى

Rabbish rah lee sadree Wa yassir leee amree Wahlul 'uqdatan milli saanee Yafqahoo qawlee

"O my Lord! Open my chest for me and make my task easy for meand make loose the knot from my tongue so that they understand my speech."

Qur'an 20:25-28

A du'a to tackle any problem

5

أَنِّى مَسَّنِيَ ٱلضُّرُّ وَأَنتَ أَرْحَمُ ٱلرَّٰحِمِينَ

Annee massaniyad durru wa Anta arhamur raahimeen

"Indeed distress has befallen me, and You are the most merciful of the merciful."

Qur'an 21:83

A dua'a asking Allah (swt) to ease hardships and sickness

6

إِنَّ ٱللَّهَ هُوَ رَبِّى وَرَبُّكُمْ فَٱعْبُدُوهُ هَـٰذَا صِرَٰطٌ مُّسْتَقِيمٌ

*Innal laaha Huwa Rabbee wa
Rabbukum fa'budooh; haaza
Siraatum Mustaqeem*

"Indeed, Allah is my Lord and your
Lord, so worship Him. This is a
straight path."

Qur'an 43:64

A du'a for Allah's (swt) help in
everyday life

7

سُبْحَٰنَ رَبِّنَآ إِنَّا كُنَّا ظَٰلِمِينَ

Subhaana rabbinaaa innaa kunnaa zaalimeen

"Exalted is our Lord! Indeed, we were wrongdoers."

Qur'an 68:29

A du'a asking for Allah (swt) to show His mercy and remove difficulties

Oppression

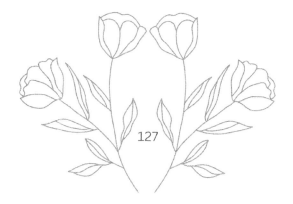

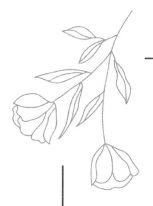

1

رَبَّنَا ٱفْتَحْ بَيْنَنَا وَبَيْنَ قَوْمِنَا بِٱلْحَقِّ وَأَنتَ خَيْرُ ٱلْفَٰتِحِينَ

Rabbanaf-tah bainana wa baina qawmina bil haqqi wa anta Khairul Fatiheen

"Our Lord, decide between us and our people in truth, and You are the best of those who give decision."

Qur'an 7:89

A dua'a when faced with oppression

2

رَبَّنَآ إِنَّنَا نَخَافُ أَن يَفۡرُطَ عَلَيۡنَآ أَوۡ أَن يَطۡغَىٰ

Rabbanaaa innanaa nakhaafu ai yafruta
'alainaaa aw ai yatghaa

"Our Lord, indeed we are afraid that he
will hasten [punishment] against us or
that he will transgress."

Qur'an 20:45

A dua'a asking for Allah (swt) to help us
stand up against injustice

Death

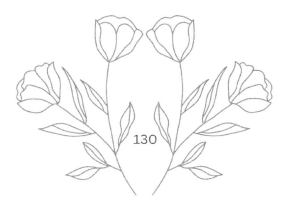

1

رَبَّنَآ أَفْرِغْ عَلَيْنَا صَبْرًا وَتَوَفَّنَا مُسْلِمِينَ

Rabbanaaa afrigh 'alainaa sabranw
wa tawaffanaa muslimeen

"Our Lord, pour upon us patience and let us die as Muslims [in submission to You]."

Qur'an 7:126

A dua'a asking Allah (swt) for sabr, perseverance, and a righteous death

Entrusting your affairs to Allah

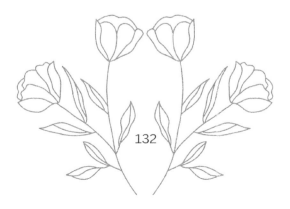

1

حَسۡبِیَ ٱللَّهُ لَآ إِلَٰهَ إِلَّا هُوَ ۖ عَلَیۡهِ تَوَكَّلۡتُ ۖ وَهُوَ رَبُّ ٱلۡعَرۡشِ ٱلۡعَظِیمِ

*Hasbiyal laahu laaa ilaaha illaa Huwa
'alaihi tawakkkaltu wa Huwa Rabbul
'Arshil 'Azeem*

"Sufficient for me is Allah; there is no
deity except Him. On Him I have relied,
and He is the Lord of the Great Throne."

Qur'an 9:129

A dua'a entrusting your affairs to Allah
(swt)

2

إِنِّى تَوَكَّلْتُ عَلَى ٱللَّهِ رَبِّى وَرَبِّكُمْ ۚ مَّا مِن دَآبَّةٍ إِلَّا هُوَ ءَاخِذٌۢ بِنَاصِيَتِهَآ ۚ إِنَّ رَبِّى عَلَىٰ صِرَٰطٍ مُّسْتَقِيمٍ

Innee tawakkaltu 'alallaahi Rabbee wa Rabbikum; maa min daaabbatin illaa Huwa aakhizum binaasiyatihaa; inna Rabbee 'alaa Siraatim mustaqeem

"Indeed, I have relied upon Allah, my Lord and your Lord. There is no creature but that He holds its forelock. Indeed, my Lord is on a path [that is] straight."

Qur'an 11:56

A dua'a entrusting your affairs to Allah (swt)

3

رَبَّنَآ إِنَّكَ تَعْلَمُ مَا نُخْفِي وَمَا نُعْلِنُ ۗ وَمَا يَخْفَىٰ عَلَى ٱللَّهِ مِن شَىْءٍ فِى ٱلْأَرْضِ وَلَا فِى ٱلسَّمَآءِ

Rabbanaaa innaka ta'lamu maa nukhfee wa maa nu'lin; wa maa yakhfaa 'alal laahi min shai'in fil ardi wa laa fis samaaa

"Our Lord, indeed You know what we conceal and what we declare, and nothing is hidden from Allah on the earth or in the heaven."

Qur'an 14:38

A dua'a showing complete trust and reliance on Allah (swt)

4

رَّبَّنَا عَلَيْكَ تَوَكَّلْنَا وَإِلَيْكَ أَنَبْنَا وَإِلَيْكَ ٱلْمَصِيرُ

*Rabbanaa 'alaika tawakkalnaa wa
ilaika anabnaa wa ilaikal maseer*

"Our Lord, upon You we have relied,
and to You we have returned, and to
You is the destination."

Qur'an 60:4

A du'a affirming reliance and trust on
Allah (swt) alone

Gratitude

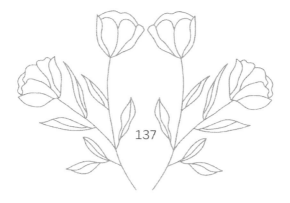

1

ٱلْحَمْدُ لِلَّهِ رَبِّ ٱلْعَٰلَمِينَ

Alhamdu lillaahi Rabbil 'aalameen

"Praise to Allah, Lord of the worlds!"

Qur'an 10:10

A dua'a showing gratitude

Travelling

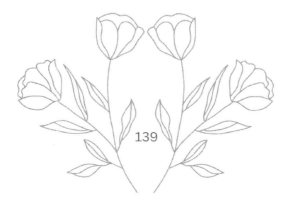

1

أَرْكَبُوا۟ فِيهَا بِسْمِ ٱللَّهِ مَجْرٮٰهَا وَمُرْسَٮٰهَآ إِنَّ رَبِّى لَغَفُورٌ رَّحِيمٌ

Ar kaboo feehaa bismil laahi
majraihaa wa mursaahaa; inna
Rabbee la Ghafoorur Raheem

"Embark therein; in the name of Allah
is its course and its anchorage.
Indeed, my Lord is Forgiving and
Merciful."

Qur'an 11:41

A dua'a for when you are travelling

2

رَّبِّ أَدْخِلْنِى مُدْخَلَ صِدْقٍ وَأَخْرِجْنِى مُخْرَجَ صِدْقٍ وَٱجْعَل لِّى مِن لَّدُنكَ سُلْطَٰنًا نَّصِيرًا

Rabbi adkhilnee mudkhala sidqinw wa akhrijnee mukhraja sidqinw waj'al lee milladunka sultaanan naseeraa

"My Lord, cause me to enter a sound entrance and to exit a sound exit and grant me from Yourself a supporting authority."

Qur'an 17:80

A dua'a for when you are travelling

3

رَّبِّ أَنزِلْنِى مُنزَلًا مُّبَارَكًا وَأَنتَ خَيْرُ ٱلْمُنزِلِينَ

Rabbi anzilnee munzalam mubaarakanw wa Anta khairul munzileen

"My Lord, let me land at a blessed landing place, and You are the best to accommodate [us]."

Qur'an 23:29

A du'a asking for travelling

4

سُبْحَٰنَ ٱلَّذِى سَخَّرَ لَنَا هَٰذَا وَمَا كُنَّا لَهُۥ مُقْرِنِينَ

Subhaanal lazee sakhkhara lana haaza wa maa kunnaa lahoo muqrineen

"Exalted is He who has subjected this to us, and we could not have [otherwise] subdued it."

Qur'an 43:13

A du'a for travelling

Residence

1

رَبِّ ٱجْعَلْ هَٰذَا ٱلْبَلَدَ ءَامِنًا وَٱجْنُبْنِى وَبَنِىَّ أَن نَّعْبُدَ ٱلْأَصْنَامَ

Rabbij 'al haazal balada aaminanw wajnubnee wa baniyya an na'budal asnaam

"My Lord, make this city [Makkah] secure and keep me and my sons away from worshipping idols."

Qur'an 14:35

A dua'a for peace in the city

Freedom from Daijal

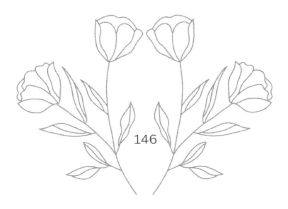

1

ٱلْحَمْدُ لِلَّهِ ٱلَّذِىٓ أَنزَلَ عَلَىٰ عَبْدِهِ ٱلْكِتَٰبَ وَلَمْ يَجْعَل لَّهُۥ عِوَجَاۜ قَيِّمًا لِّيُنذِرَ بَأْسًا شَدِيدًا مِّن لَّدُنْهُ وَيُبَشِّرَ ٱلْمُؤْمِنِينَ ٱلَّذِينَ يَعْمَلُونَ ٱلصَّٰلِحَٰتِ أَنَّ لَهُمْ أَجْرًا حَسَنًا

Alhamdu lillaahil lazeee anzala 'alaa 'abdihil kitaaba wa lam yaj'al lahoo 'iwajaa Qaiyimal liyunzira ba'asan shadeedam mil ladunhu wa yubashshiral mu'mineenal lazeena ya'maloonas saalihaati anna lahum ajran hasanaa

"[All] praise is [due] to Allah, who has sent down upon His Servant the Book and has not made therein any deviance. [He has made it] straight, to warn of severe punishment from Him and to give good tidings to the believers who do righteous deeds that they will have a good reward."

Qur'an 18:1-2

A dua'a to be free from Daijal's grip

Increase in Knowledge

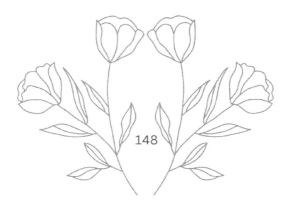

1

رَّبِّ زِدْنِى عِلْمًا

Rabbi zidnee 'ilmaa

"My Lord, increase me in knowledge."

Qur'an 20:114

A dua'a asking for Allah (swt) for an increase in knowledge

2

رَبِّ هَبْ لِى حُكْمًا وَأَلْحِقْنِى بِالصَّلِحِينَ

*Rabbi hab lee hukmanw wa
alhiqnee bis saaliheen*

"My Lord, grant me authority
and join me with the right."

Qur'an 26:83

A du'a asking for wisdom

Marriage

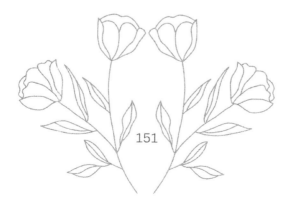

1

رَبَّنَا هَبْ لَنَا مِنْ أَزْوَٰجِنَا وَذُرِّيَّٰتِنَا قُرَّةَ أَعْيُنٍ وَٱجْعَلْنَا لِلْمُتَّقِينَ إِمَامًا

Rabbanaa hab lanaa min azwaajinaa wa zurriyaatinaa qurrata a'yuninw waj 'alnaa lilmuttaqeena Imaamaa

"Our Lord, grant us from among our wives and offspring comfort to our eyes and make us a leader [i.e., example] for the righteous."

Qur'an 25:74

A du'a asking Allah (swt) for calmness, joy or happiness among our spouses and through our children and future generations and to be a good leader and role model for the righteous

Fulfilment

of

needs

1

رَبِّ إِنِّي لِمَآ أَنزَلْتَ إِلَيَّ مِنْ خَيْرٍ فَقِيرٌ

Rabbi innee limaaa anzalta ilaiya min khairin faqeer

"My Lord, indeed I am, for whatever good You would send down to me, in need."

Qur'an 28:24

A du'a asking Allah (swt) to fulfil your needs

Rain

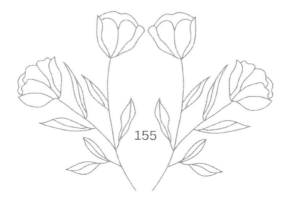

1

اللّٰهُ الَّذِي يُرْسِلُ الرِّيَاحَ فَتُثِيرُ سَحَابًا فَيَبْسُطُهُ فِي السَّمَاءِ كَيْفَ يَشَاءُ وَيَجْعَلُهُ كِسَفًا فَتَرَى الْوَدْقَ يَخْرُجُ مِنْ خِلَالِهِ فَإِذَا أَصَابَ بِهِ مَن يَشَاءُ مِنْ عِبَادِهِ إِذَا هُمْ يَسْتَبْشِرُونَ وَإِن كَانُوا مِن قَبْلِ أَن يُنَزَّلَ عَلَيْهِم مِّن قَبْلِهِ لَمُبْلِسِينَ فَانظُرْ إِلَى آثَارِ رَحْمَتِ اللّٰهِ كَيْفَ يُحْيِ الْأَرْضَ بَعْدَ مَوْتِهَا إِنَّ ذَٰلِكَ لَمُحْيِ الْمَوْتَىٰ وَهُوَ عَلَىٰ كُلِّ شَيْءٍ قَدِيرٌ

Allaahul lazee yursilur riyaaha fatuseeru sahaaban fa yabsutuhoo fis samaaa'i kaifa yashaaa'u wa yaj'aluhoo kisafan fatoral wadqa yakhruju min khilaalihee fa izaaa asaaba bihee mai yashaaa'u min 'ibaadiheee izaa hum yastabshiroon. Wa in kaanoo min qabli any yunazzala 'alaihim min qablihee lamubliseen. Fanzur ilaaa aasaari rahmatil laahi kaifa yuhyil arda ba'da mawtihaa; inna zaalika lamuhyil mawtaa wa Huwa 'alaa kulli shai'in Qadeer

"It is Allah who sends the winds, and they stir the clouds and spread them in the sky however He wills, and He makes them fragments so you see the rain emerge from within them. And when He causes it to fall upon whom He wills of His servants, immediately they rejoice. Although they were, before it was sent down upon them – before that, in despair. So observe the effects of the mercy of Allah - how He gives life to the earth after its lifelessness. Indeed, that [same one] will give life to the dead, and He is over all things competent."

Qur'an 30:48-50

A du'a for rain

Dua Praising Allah

1

رَبَّنَآ إِنَّكَ رَءُوفٌ رَّحِيمٌ

Rabbannaaa innaka Ra'oofur Raheem

"Our Lord, indeed You are Kind and Merciful."

Qur'an 59:10

A du'a praising Allah (swt)

Interview

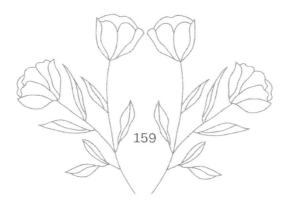

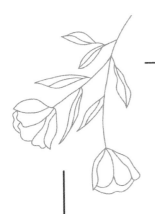

1

رَبِّ ٱشۡرَحۡ لِى صَدۡرِى وَيَسِّرۡ لِىٓ أَمۡرِى وَٱحۡلُلۡ عُقۡدَةً مِّن لِّسَانِى يَفۡقَهُوا۟ قَوۡلِى

Rabbish rah lee sadree Wa yassir leee amree Wahlul 'uqdatan milli saanee Yafqahoo qawlee

"O my Lord! Open my chest for me and make my task easy for meand make loose the knot from my tongue so that they understand my speech."

Qur'an 20:25-28

A du'a to tackle any problem

Printed in Great Britain
by Amazon

45801134R00091